Helpful Dogs

by Caroline Burke

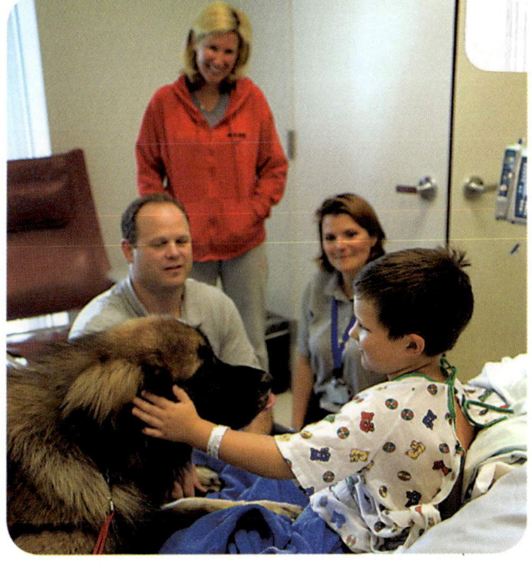

Scott Foresman
is an imprint of

Glenview, Illinois • Boston, Massachusetts • Mesa, Arizona
Shoreview, Minnesota • Upper Saddle River, New Jersey

Photographs
Every effort has been made to secure permission and provide appropriate credit for photographic material. The publisher deeply regrets any omission and pledges to correct errors called to its attention in subsequent editions.

Unless otherwise acknowledged, all photographs are the property of Pearson Education, Inc.

3 ©PA/Topham/The Image Works, Inc.; 4 ©Lehtikuva Oy/Sakki/Rex Features, Limited; 5 ©Dan Rosenstrauch/Zuma Press, Inc.; 6 ©Penny Tweedie/Photo Researchers, Inc.; 7 ©Manuel Balce Ceneta/AP Images; 8 ©Marmaduke St. John/Alamy

ISBN 13: 978-0-328-39374-9
ISBN 10:   0-328-39374-6

1 2 3 4 5 6 7 8 9 10 V010 17 16 15 14 13 12 11 10 09 08

Dogs can go to special schools.
Dogs can learn to help people.

The dog can help open a door.

Dogs can help people in wheelchairs.
First the dog opens the door.
Then the dog turns on the light.

Dogs can help people who cannot see.
"Shall we go to school?" the girl asks.
Her dog helps her cross the street.

Dogs can help people who cannot hear.
Dogs can let people know when babies cry.
Dogs can even learn sign language!

Dogs can help children read.
The boy bought a book.
The boy reads to the dog.
The boy is not scared to make mistakes.

Dogs can help people in hospitals.
Dogs can make the hospital stay pleasant.
Dogs can make people's lives happy.